Comn

How To Speak Effectively and Improve Your Relationships, Problem Solving, Listening, and Social Skills

Table of Contents

Table of Contents..
Introduction..
Overcoming Obstacles..
Determining your Goals...
Five Questions of Effective Communication...
Develop Self-Confidence to Communicate Effectively....................................
The Art of Small Talk...
Gulp! I have to Give a Presentation..
Communicating Through Letter Writing..
Hostile Communication...
Fitting All the Pieces Together...
Conclusion..

Introduction

Have you ever felt like you failed miserably when you try to communicate? If so, then you definitely need this book. It is filled with the research that you need to communicate effectively. Remember that communication takes on many different forms both verbal and non-verbal. It is vital to understand both forms before you try to communicate. After you have mastered the techniques in this book, you will be better able to deliver your message.

As we take the journey through this book, you will learn many new things and be reminded of other things that you already know. You will learn the questions that you need to ask in order to communicate effectively. Much of your success in communicating effectively is based on your self-confidence so we have provided tips to help you develop the confidence that you need.

Communication is about much more than simply exchanging information. You must understand the emotions and intentions behind that information. You must be able to convey your message so that it is fully received and understood exactly as you intended. However, you must also be able to listen and gain the full meaning of the information being given to you so that other people feel heard and understood. Lack of these skills can be barriers between you and others that continue the cycle of misunderstandings, frustrations and conflicts. You will be warned about these barriers to effective communication and how to overcome them.

Everyone has to communicate in a variety of situations. Therefore, this book explores how to communicate at networking events including things you need to do before, during and after those events. At some point, almost everyone must give a presentation. Yet many people are afraid of giving a presentation, so we provide you with important tips that make giving those presentations easier. Not all communication is verbal so we will help you to conquer the art of letter writing.

Unfortunately, not all messages are positive. At some point, you will need to give a hostile message to someone. Following the techniques outlined in this book allows you to make sure that your message gets through.

It is important that your body delivers the same message as your words. Therefore, you need to conquer the art of gesturing, body language, eye contact and personal appearance.

Effective communication will help you to strengthen your relationships with others. It will improve your ability to work with a team, make decisions and solve problems. Having effective communication skills will enable you to present all information, even the negative or difficult messages, without creating conflict or destroying trust. It really is the glue that holds everything together.

Many people believe that because they can speak it means that they can communicate effectively. However, effective communication is a learned skill. Despite that, it is much more effective when it is spontaneous rather than when delivered by rote. For example, if you are giving a speech and simply read it from the notes you've made it will rarely have the same impact as if you appeared to deliver it 'off the cuff'. It takes time and effort to develop your skills and become an effective communicator. However, the more effort and practice you put in, the more natural your communication skills will become.

Come on this journey with us!

Overcoming Obstacles

Before you can improve your communication skills, you must know what obstacles you may encounter and need to overcome. This is what this chapter will address while the following chapters will help you to improve on the skills you may already possess.

"Say what you mean." That sounds so simple, doesn't it? But it's easier said than done. It may be a cliché, but it's a cliché for a reason. All too often what we are trying to communicate gets lost in translation, no matter our intentions.

For example, you are quitting your job and you tell your boss that you think you must hand in your two weeks notice. Now your **intent** is to tell your boss that you *are* handing in your two weeks notice. However, your boss hears that you are only *thinking* about handing in your notice.

Do you see what happened there? In this scenario, you failed to communicate properly that you were quitting and your boss simply thought you were letting him know you were unhappy with the way things were. This is a scenario that you set up that will cause frustration and conflict between you and your boss.

So how do you fix this? You fix it by improving your communication skills and recognizing the barriers to effective communication.

Barriers to Effective Communication

- *Stress.* When you are stressed or overwhelmed emotionally you are more likely to misunderstand other people. This leads to you sending confusing or off-putting nonverbal signals and falling into poor patterns of behavior. This in turn can lead to conflicts of varying degrees from confusion to vehement arguments. If you find this happening, you need to take a moment or two so that you can calm down before continuing the conversation.

- *Lack of focus.* If you are multitasking, you aren't able to communicate effectively. You will miss vital nonverbal cues in the conversation if you are planning what you are going to say next, checking text messages, thinking about other tasks you have to do or even daydreaming due to boredom or disinterest in the topic of discussion. It is imperative that you stay focused on the experience as it is happening.

- *Inconsistent body language.* Your nonverbal communication should reinforce what you are saying, not contradict it. As an example, you cannot say 'yes' to something while frowning or shaking your head 'no'. Having conflicting verbal and nonverbal communication will probably make your listener feel like you are being dishonest.

- *Negative body language.* This may seem like it is part of inconsistent body language but it really isn't. If you really disagree with what is being said, it will show if you are not very careful. Perhaps you dislike the person conveying the message, that too can show through in your nonverbal cues. The most common forms of negative body language are crossing your arms, tapping of fingers or feet and avoiding eye contact. However, it can be something you don't even realize you are doing; such as, heaving sighs, eye rolling, or even making tsking sounds. You don't have to agree with what is being said or like the person saying it. However, in order to communicate effectively, you must be able to listen without making the other person defensive. To do this, you must avoid sending negative signals.

People often focus on what they should say. Effective communication is more about listening than talking. When you listen well, you will not only understand the information being offered but will also understand the emotions the speaker is communicating.

There is a difference between simply hearing what is being said and engaged listening. When you are engaged with what is being said you will hear the subtle tones of the speakers voice. Hearing those tones will tell you how the speaker is feeling and the emotions they are trying to convey. You will make the speaker feel heard and understood which will help to build a stronger relationship between you and the other person.

You will find that being able to communicate in this way that you will experience less stress. As an example, if the person you are talking to is calm then you will be calm as well. Similarly, if you are speaking to someone who is agitated, you will be able to help them calm down if you listen attentively and make them feel understood.

Become an Engaged Listener

You should want to fully understand and connect with other people. If this is the case then listening in an engaged way will come naturally to you. If you struggle with this, try the following tips. The more you practice, the more satisfying your interactions with others will become.

- *Focus on the speaker.* This means not only words but also body language, tone of voice and other nonverbal cues. The tone of voice will convey the speakers emotions. If you are thinking about other things, checking text messages or doodling out of boredom you will definitely miss the nonverbal cues and the emotional content behind the words. If you find it difficult to concentrate on certain topics, try repeating the speakers words in your head. This will reinforce their message and help you stay focused on them.

- *Favor your right ear.* The left side of our brains contain the primary processing centers for both speech comprehension and emotions. Favoring your right ear can help you detect the emotional nuances better since the left side of the brain is connected to the right side of the body. In order to do this, keep your posture straight, your chin a little lower than you might usually hold it and tilt your right ear toward the speaker. This will help you to pick up the emotional content of the speakers words.

- *Avoid interrupting or redirecting.* This may seem like common sense but it is more than simply cutting into something the other person is saying. Listening is not the same as simply waiting for your turn to speak. You aren't going to be able to concentrate on what is being said if you are thinking about what you will be saying next. Many times the other person will read your facial expressions and know that you are thinking about something else.

- *Show your interest.* You can do this by smiling at the speaker, nod once in a while and by making sure that your posture is open and inviting. You want to encourage the other person to continue with short comments like 'yes' or 'uh huh'. However, be aware that this can easily backfire if you are not careful. Do you remember what was said earlier about not being able to listen if you are multitasking? For example, you are sitting on the couch at home watching your favorite TV show or sports team and your spouse or child comes to speak to you. For the first few moments of the conversation, you manage to focus on the discussion but something happens on the TV that pulls your attention away from the one talking to you. The next thing you know your spouse is storming out angrily or you find that you have agreed to something because your kid took advantage of your distraction.

- *Set aside personal judgment.* To communicate effectively doesn't mean you have to like other people or agree with their ideas. However, you do need to put your personal judgment aside and withhold criticism on their values or opinions in order to fully understand a person. Once you are able to do this, you will find that can lead to a profound connection with other people.

- *Provide feedback.* If you find that you are not comprehending exactly what the other person is saying, you can ask for clarification by reflecting a paraphrase of what you did understand. You can do this by beginning your reflection with "What I'm hearing is ..." or "Sounds like you are saying ...". If you simply repeat what the speaker has said exactly, you will sound unintelligent or insincere. You want to express what the other person's words meant to you. Another good way to request clarification on certain points is to ask "What do you mean when you say ..." or "Is this what you mean?"

You can improve your listening abilities by increasing the muscle tone of the muscles of the middle ear as well. This will allow you to detect the higher frequencies that occur in human speech which are where you will hear the emotional message being offered. Focusing your attention on what someone is saying is good exercise for those tiny muscles. However, singing, playing a wind instrument like the flute, clarinet or oboe, and listening to high-frequency classical music with violins rather than the low-frequency rock or rap music are also good exercises for the muscles of the inner ear.

Pay Attention to Nonverbal Cues

Nonverbal communication includes facial expressions, eye contact, body movement and posture, gestures, tone of voice, breathing and muscle tension as well as your mode of dress. The ways that you look, move, listen and react to other people tells them more about how you are feeling than words ever will.

By using open body language like uncrossed arms, sitting on the edge of your seat and maintaining eye contact you will be able to enhance effective communication. Patting a friend on the back while complimenting them or pounding your fists can help to emphasize your verbal message. These are part of that nonverbal portion of communication that helps you and others to understand all of what is being said.

By improving your ability to understand and use nonverbal cues you will be able to connect with other people, express what you really mean, navigate your way through difficult situations and build better relationships in any situation you may find yourself.

- Be aware of individual differences. You must take into account that age, religion, gender, culture and emotional states affect people's body language. An

American teenager, a grieving widow from Russia and a businessman from Japan will all use different nonverbal signals.

- Look at nonverbal communication signals as a group. You don't want to read too much into just one gesture or nonverbal cue. You want to consider all of the nonverbal cues you receive and give, from tone of voice to eye contact to body language, from the person speaking. Brief lapses where eye contact slips or arms cross unconsciously can happen to anyone. Therefore, if you consider the signals as a group, you will get a better 'read' on the speaker.

- Use nonverbal signals that match your words. As stated before, nonverbal communication is supposed to reinforce what is being said rather than contradicting it. If you say one thing but your body language or tone says the opposite, your listener will feel like you are being dishonest. This can cause them to entirely discount the information you are trying to impart but it can also cause them to distrust everything that you say in the future.

- Adjust your nonverbal cues to your audience. The tone of your voice will be different when you are addressing children than it will be when you are addressing adults. You must also take into account the emotional states and cultural backgrounds of the people you are interacting with as well.

- Be positive no matter what. You can convey positive body language even when you are not actually experiencing positive feelings. For example, if you are nervous about a situation you can still show the absolute opposite. This process is called 'fake it till you make it'. Pretend you have a job interview and you are nervous. Would you walk with your head down? Would you avoid eye contact with the interviewer? Would you mumble a greeting and offer a limp handshake? You can 'fake it till you make it' by walking tall with your shoulders back, smile at your interviewer and maintain eye contact as well as offering a firm handshake. This will put the other person at ease and help you to feel more confident at the same time.

Keep Stress in Check

In order to communicate effectively, you must be aware of your emotions and remain in control of them. This means you must learn how to manage stress. Misunderstandings happen when you and others send confusing nonverbal signals which can cause you or your listeners to be put off or to begin reacting with unhealthy patterns of behavior.

How many times have you regretted saying or doing something because you were stressed over a disagreement? If you are like most people your answer is probably more than you can count, correct? You can avoid such regrets by being able to relieve that stress quickly so that you return to a calmer state of mind. Oftentimes you will be able to calm the other person as well. Only when you are calm and relaxed can you know whether or not the discussion you are having requires a response or whether it would be better to remain silent. These are all predicated on the nonverbal signals the other person is giving.

There are many ways that you can work on relieving stress so that you can communicate more effectively. Controlling stress will allow you to manage your emotions and think on your feet when you are under pressure. Follow these tips to help yourself stay calm when you are under pressure.

- *Use stalling tactics*. This will give you time to think. You can ask to have a question repeated or you can request clarification of a particular statement before you respond.

- *Pause*. Being silent isn't always a bad thing. It allows you to collect your thoughts. Doing so will make you seem more in control which is always better than rushing a response and coming across as less than competent.

- *Make points singly*. If you have several points that you must get across, make each point individually. If you waffle from one point to another in a random fashion you risk losing the interest of your audience. Make a point and offer an example so that you can gauge your listener's reaction to be sure they are ready for the next point you need to make.

- *Provide a clear delivery*. How you say things is just as important as what you say. First, you need to speak clearly. Mumbling or slurring your speech comes across as informal and inconsiderate of your listeners. Second, make sure you keep eye contact as much as possible. This tells your listener that you are interested in and focused on them and their needs at that moment. Third, maintain an even tone of voice. This doesn't mean speak in a monotone, it simply means that if you start with an excited or welcoming tone of voice then you should continue that tone until you are at a point where the conversation deserves a change in tone. And fourth, you need to keep your body language open and relaxed. This will show your audience that you are willing to listen to their idea or opinion within your conversation.

- *Summarize and stop*. This is it, literally. Wrap up the information with a summary and then stop. Even if it leaves a silence in the room, once the information has been delivered then it is time to stop talking. Remember that silence is not always a bad thing.

If you find that a conversation is starting to raise tempers you will need something that will bring the emotional tension down quickly. Learning to reduce stress while in the moment, you will be able to face any strong emotion you are experiencing and behave appropriately in each situation. When you are able to maintain a relaxed and energized state of awareness you will be able to remain emotionally available and engaged with your listeners even when something upsetting happens in the course of conversation. The tips below will help you to deal with stress during communication.

- *Recognize you are becoming stressed.* Are your stomach muscles tight or sore? Are your hands clenching into fists? Are you forgetting to breathe or are your breaths shallow? These are all ways that your body tells you that you are stressed while you are communicating. Recognizing these signs will help you deal with the stress and return to a relaxed and calm state of communication.

- *Pause.* As shown above, this allows you to collect your thoughts. However, it also gives you a moment to calm yourself before you decide to continue the conversation or if it would be better to postpone it.

- *Quickly manage stress.* You can bring your senses to your rescue to help you alleviate stress in the moment. The best way to rapidly relieve stress is through your senses of sight, sound, touch, taste and smell. You can take a few deep breaths, clench and relax muscles or recall an enjoyable, sensory-rich memory. However, each person will respond differently to sensory input so you will need to find something that is soothing to you.

- *Be humorous*. You want to look for humor in the current situation. If you use it appropriately, humor is a very good way to relieve stress when you are communicating. This is why public speakers will have an ice breaker at the start of their speech. When you or those around you begin to take things too seriously, you can lighten the mood by sharing an amusing story or a joke. Once tensions are reduced then you can continue where you left off.

- *Compromise*. You must be willing to compromise, that's what life is all about. If you and the person you are speaking with can bend a little, you will find a happy middle ground that will reduce stress for everyone involved. If the other person cares much more about a topic than you do, a compromise may be the easiest thing for you to do. It might also be a good investment in your future relationship with that person.

- *Agree to disagree*. Sometimes it is necessary to step away from a situation to allow everyone to calm down. Go for a walk outside or spend a few minutes in meditation if you need to. Doing something physical or finding a quiet place so that you can regain your mental balance will help you reduce stress quickly. The few minutes away from the situation that caused that stress will allow you to return to the conversation in a much calmer frame of mind so that you can resolve any problem that may have arisen during that interchange.

Be Assertive

Assertive and direct expression of your thoughts keeps communication clear and can boost your self-esteem and decision making abilities. Being assertive must be done in an open and honest way when you express your feelings, thoughts or needs while standing up for yourself. To do this, you must remember to respect others as you do so without being rude or hostile. Unfortunately, assertiveness is often confused with aggressiveness because the person being assertive does so *without* being respectful of others at the same time. Effectively communicating through assertiveness is not about forcing your opinion on someone else or winning an argument. The following list will help you to improve your assertiveness.

- *Value yourself*. You are important. Unfortunately, many people do not believe this of themselves because others have demeaned and discounted them for so long. Your ideas and your opinions are just as important as anyone else's.

- *Express negative thoughts in a positive way*. It is perfectly fine to be angry. However, you must be respectful while you express those thoughts at the same time. Failure to show that respect to another person while trying to tell them that you are upset and what exactly upset you can cause even worse problems for you. Lack of respect for others often leads to placing blame, name-calling and, sometimes, outright hatred which will lead to loss of a relationship.

- *Receive all feedback positively.* This is often the most difficult for anyone to learn and implement. It is often associated with self-esteem issues. You need to accept compliments graciously, learn from your mistakes and ask for help when you need it.

- *Learn to say no.* You need to know your limits and not let others take advantage of you. It can be difficult to develop this skill if you have previously been the one to accept any 'job' even if it overwhelmed you. You will need to start looking for alternatives when you must say no so that everyone will feel good about the outcome.

Being assertive takes time. Not only for yourself to get used to being assertive but also for those you interact with and who are probably not used to the new you.

When you show sensitivity to the other person, you are exhibiting empathetic assertion. To practice this, you will recognize the other person's feelings or situation before making your needs or opinions known. For example, you can say "I know you've been very busy at work, but I want you to make time for us as well." when asking a friend or family member to spend more time with you.

Perhaps you have been having a difficult time getting your kids, boss or coworkers. If your first attempts at being assertive do not succeed, you may need to become increasingly firm as time passes which might include consequences if your needs are not met. With a child you may say, "If you do not clean your room, I will be forced to take away your computer privileges." With a boss or coworker it may be more along the lines of, "If you don't abide by the contract, I'll be forced to pursue legal action."

Wherever you are in assertive behavior, you can always practice being assertive. Beginning in low risk situations and finding success there will help to build your confidence and allow you to move up to higher risk situations. If you have just chosen to be more assertive, you might ask friends or family members to allow you to practice the suggested assertiveness techniques on them first.

Determining your Goals

Everyone communicates in some way with every person that they come in contact with on a daily basis. In some situations, that is simply to look the other way as you pass an old enemy on the street; while in other situations, it is to hold someone tightly in your arms and embrace them. Your ability to communicate effectively is key to success in life. It is particularly essential in the workplace where effective communication can make the difference between being promoted and being fired.

The first step in communicating effectively is to have a predetermined communication goal. The first step in setting up a communication goal is to determine what needs to be communicated and why.

Stop for a moment and imagine that you are preparing for a car trip. There are very few people who can hop in a car and just take off. Instead, you must first choose a destination so that you will know when you have arrived. Then, you must decide on what roads you need to take to get to your destination. You will need to know a rough estimate of the miles that you will cover, so that you can budget accordingly for the trip. Taking care of all the little details before you leave home ensures that your trip is successful.

It is no different when you are going to communicate with someone. You need to start out by deciding where you are going with your communication. Therefore, you must have an overall goal. Each communication should advance your plan to achieve your goals. So, if you have not already done so, start by creating a list of goals in your life.

As life coach Myrko Thum says, "A goal is a thought with commitment to make it real." The first step in doing this is to get in a place where you can allow yourself to dream. Numerous research studies suggest that this is easier to do when you are outside, but regardless of where you are at you must feel free to dream without fearing interruption and without feeling that you will be judged by anyone.

Now, that you are in your happy place, start to write down ideas about goals just as fast as you can possibly write. You are not judging the ideas at this point, but simply writing them down. If you find that you are having trouble coming up with ideas, then try dividing your life up into different areas. Your list should be as unique as you are, but it might include your mind, your body, your soul, and your profession.

Now, that you have brainstormed a list of possible goals, then go back and list those goals by priority. Again, this list should be unique. Do not let anyone choose the list for you, even in your own mind. It is simply amazing that only three percent of the population has ever written out their life goals, but simply float through life. When you understand your life goals, you instantly become a better communicator, because you understand how your communication affects those goals.

Now, concentrate on the very first goal. What steps do you need to take to achieve that goal? Make another list that puts the steps that you need to achieve that goal in order. Now, you are ready to take that very first step and break it down into even smaller steps.

In order to do this, you can employ the SMART and/or the CLEAR methods to help you further detail that list of goals.

What is the SMART method?

The SMART system has been considered the best-practice framework for setting goals. It is often used by employers during performance reviews and to allow the employee to know exactly what is required for achieving success.

- *Specific*. Your goals must be clear and unambiguous. This is to make sure you know exactly what you are wanting to accomplish. Returning to the idea of a car trip, if you do not know where you are going it is impossible to determine if you have reached your destination.

- *Measurable.* Your results need to be able to be measured in some way. If you are using this method to get a promotion, you might use the number of products sold each week or a completion percentage. If you are using this method for physical fitness, you may use the number of pounds you can bench press or the number of blocks or miles you can walk, run or bike.

- *Attainable.* Your goals must be realistic, not just to you but to others as well. If it seems unattainable to others you may not receive the support you need or deserve. If it seems unattainable to you, you may feel discouraged and give up. Researchers know that people are much more motivated to work on goals that they actually see as achievable, so do not frustrate yourself by choosing goals that are not achievable.

- *Relevant.* Your goals should relate to what you are using that list of goals for. If it is for your career, your list of goals should reflect that relevance. For example, a writer wouldn't set a goal of baking 1000 cupcakes by 3pm if it is 9am. While a writer can bake, it would take a professional baker to create 1000 cupcakes in six hours. A more relevant goal for the writer would be to write 1000 words per hour. In order to determine if a goal is relevant, ask yourself these questions: Is it in **your** control to achieve it? Is it realistic for you to achieve? Is it worthwhile? Is it the right time for this change to be implemented? Do you have the skills necessary to achieve this goal? When asking these questions, if you get a "no" response, then you need to back up and examine the earlier steps to create a more relevant goal.

- *Time-bound*. You should have definite beginning and ending points for each goal on your list. Each goal should have a fixed duration so that you don't procrastinate. Procrastination is the mortal enemy of success.

With the SMART method, relevancy will be the step that takes the most time to determine. This is because of the amount of adjusting of goals you will need to do in order to be able to answer 'yes' to every single question you ask about whether or not the goal is relevant.

If some of the requirements of a specific goal are outside of your control, it is less likely that you will actually achieve that goal. If some portion of the goal is outside of your control, you may need to back up and acquire those resources first. Sometimes, it is simply a case of saving up money, which may be your first step in achieving the goal, but at other times, it may be positioning yourself to share the idea with someone in power or moving to a new company where your goals will be embraced.

Some goals seem realistic but when you really begin looking at the particulars that will be required to reach that goal, realism often goes out the window which will ultimately make that goal unattainable and therefore irrelevant.

People are much more motivated to work on goals that seem worthwhile. This varies by the individual, so what is worthwhile for one person to work on may be totally irrelevant to another.

There are many worthwhile goals, but if the time is not right, then the goal may need to be saved until later. Your goal may be very worthwhile, but if your timing is not right, then you are doomed to failure.

Everyone has their own skills. Therefore, before embarking on any goal, it is important that you choose goals that match up with your skills. You may have a great idea for an awesome painting, but if you have no painting skill, then you will probably not turn out a masterpiece.

Make sure that your goal is timely. People are much more motivated to work on a goal with a deadline. If you say that 'someday' you will achieve your goal, then that someday will never arrive. Instead, set a deadline on your goal and mark it on a calendar where you will see it on a regular basis.

What is the CLEAR method?

The CLEAR method is very similar to the SMART method but with a slight difference in how the list is created. This method is a newer one compared to the SMART method which was developed in 1981. Andrew Kreek developed the CLEAR method because he felt the SMART method was not keeping up with the faster-paced, more mobile businesses of the 21st century.

- *Collaborative*. Your goals should encourage everyone involved to work together. Even if you are a team of one, you still have your support system to cheer you on to the finish line. Ask for suggestions on how they, your supporters or your co-workers, would frame the goals on your list but make sure you are making the final decisions on what those goals will be. This way, your support system or other team members will know exactly what will be accomplished.

- *Limited*. Each goal should be limited in both scope, what is to be done during that step, and duration, how long it will take.

- *Emotional*. Your goals should tap into your team's energy and passion so that you can make an emotional connection to them. The more passionate you and your supporters or team members are about something, the more likely that goal will be accomplished.

- *Appreciable*. Large goals should be broken down into smaller goals. This is so that each goal can be accomplished quickly and easily. Doing so allows for long-term gain and raises enthusiasm as goals are accomplished and able to be checked off the list.

- *Refinable*. You want to set goals with a steadfast objective. However, as new situations and information arise you need to give yourself permission to modify and refine those goals as you go. If you fail to refine your goals you risk the chance that a goal will be unreachable.

Now, that you have set your goals, you have positioned yourself to communicate your goals with others. Look at the first goals that you have created, and ask yourself what information you need to communicate to achieve those goals. Plan those communications ahead of time to ensure that they are easy to understand. Choose the right style to communicate in since some messages are much easier to communicate in person where you can judge the other person's non-verbal clues. Other messages can easily be communicated with a phone call, as it still provides a chance for you to judge the other person's reaction though their tone of voice, without having to plan a meeting that you can both attend at the same place. Still other messages can easily be communicated via email where the other person can attend to it at their convenience though you should be aware that misunderstanding can still occur if you have not written your email out clearly.

Make sure that your communication is organized. It is usually a good idea for you make a list of the key points that you want to communicate as they relate to your goals. Making a list of these goals before you start to communicate is a great way to make sure that your communication stays on point and does not stray too far from accomplishing your goal.

When you wrote essays in high school, your teacher taught you to write great topic sentences to start the essay. The same principle applies when you are setting out to communicate about your goal. This sentence should tell the reader or listener why you are communicating with them. It should prepare the reader or listener to pay attention to what you are trying to communicate by using thought-provoking words. Additionally, this topic sentence should grab the listener's or reader's attention, so that they are prepared to hear the message that you need to communicate.

All communication should be limited to the most important points that you need to communicate to meet your first objective. Try to limit your communication to no more than three main points. This helps to keep your communication short enough that others are prepared to listen. It also helps to ensure that you are staying on the first steps of meeting your goals. Finally, it ensures that you are staying on task and not allowing the communication to wander which respects your time and the time of the other person.

Effective communication starts with determining your own life objectives. After you have determined those objectives, then it is key to break those goals down into shorter term goals. Once you have set your goals, put them in order. This allows you to know who and in what order you need to be communicating. After you have determined this vital information, then start communicating your plan in a way that is appropriate to the content that you need to deliver, that is organized, and that is limited to the information that you need at that time.

Five Questions of Effective Communication

You have written your goals, and understand the message that you need to deliver and who you need to communicate that message to in order to achieve your goals. You have also determined who you need to deliver your message to in order to meet your goals. The next step is to engage that other person in your communication.

Rudyard Kipling, the famous English short story writer, wrote "I keep six honest serving men (They taught me all I knew); Their names are What and Why and When And How and Where and Who." in the Elephant's Story. While he wrote his poem in 1902, the principles that Kipling wrote about still apply to effective communication today.

In order to have effective communication, ask yourself what information needs to be conveyed. This allows you to make sure that you are keeping your communication on track. In most cases, the person who is doing the talking tries to communicate way too much information at one time. As covered in the last chapter, before you try to communicate, make a list of no more than three main points. This assures that your communication is staying on target and helps you organize your thoughts.

You will also want to consider just why you are communicating your message. Is it to suggest a change in the way things are done or a policy that needs to be changed to keep up with modern business practices? Perhaps you are requesting more information about a topic. No matter the reason for your communication, it should tie into the objective that you are trying to accomplish at that moment. If it does not, then the timing may not be right for that communication.

Effectively communicating why you are offering those suggestions or need the information helps the other person understand why they need to give you the time that is required to answer your communication. If you cannot come up with a concrete answer to why the other person should care, then stop for a moment and ask yourself if you are asking the right person. Often times, you will discover that there is a better person that you need to communicate the information to at this moment.

If this is a business communication, there is another reason that you need to communicate the why message. Security measures need to be very tight within companies. Therefore, before asking a person to answer your communication, make sure to tell the person why you need the information to meet the goals of the company.

It is also important to answer when the right time to communicate the message is to capture the listener's attention. A common scenario illustrating this point plays out in many homes every day. As everyone is hopping into the vehicle for the drive to school, Johnny suddenly begins telling his mother that he forgot that he had to have two dollars for school. Of course, the mother has no cash on her because she always uses her debit card. She hurriedly pulls into a convenience store and finds an ATM. While she now has cash, she does not have the exact amount that Johnny needs. So, she buys a candy bar and jumps back into the vehicle. Little Johnny forgetting that the stop was for him in the beginning, sees the candy bar and starts demanding the candy. Meanwhile, the mother who is quickly losing her cool, hands Johnny the candy bar and the money.

Think how much simpler it would be if Johnny had communicated the message to his mother the night before. Of course, people expect adults to act more responsibly than Johnny did, but often adults fail to do so. Instead, stop and think about the best time to communicate the message is before delivering the message.

For example, have you ever been guilty of communicating something at the last possible moment. Not because you did not know that there was going to be a problem, but because you simply put off communicating this information. In all cases, communicating the message earlier, would have allowed the person to have time to stop and think about a solution more rationally.

If you know that the person who is going to receive the message is going to be tied up thinking about other issues, it really is not fair to the other individual to communicate the message at that time. Instead, wait until the person is ready to pay attention to your message.

It is important to consider how you are going to communicate your message. Before you start to communicate, take a second to make sure that you are clear about the message that you want to communicate. Make sure to limit yourself to three or fewer main ideas in each communication, but more importantly, make sure that you communicate all the information that you have about the situation. Never expect the person you are trying to communicate with to read between the lines.

Before you start to communicate your message, try to put yourself in the other person's shoes. Organize your communication not only so that it not only delivers an organized message, but does it as concisely as possible. If you are communicating in writing, then write a rough draft. Before sending your communication, ask if there are any filler words that you can eliminate. This assures that the person receiving the communication can deal with it in the shortest time possible and shows that you really care about the other person.

Regardless of how you are communicating, use words that your listener can understand. For example, if you are communicating with a professional in the same field, then it may be very acceptable to communicate with acronyms, however, if you are communicating with people outside your profession, then you will want to keep the use of acronyms to a minimum. Choose which words that you want to use very carefully so that they communicate your message clearly to your intended audience.

Being as concise as possible, carries an inherent danger. Being concise means keeping your communication brief but it also means sticking to the point. There is nothing an audience hates more than having to listen to a speaker ramble on and on after they've seemingly made their point. Likewise, no reader will want to struggle through a dozen sentences when fewer would do. Check over your notes or email and eliminate any adjectives or filler words you don't really need. You can often delete words like 'for instance', 'you see', 'definitely', 'kind of', 'literally', 'basically', and 'I mean'. Make sure there are no unnecessary sentences, which are usually repeating your point in different words multiple ways. Besides sticking to the point and not rambling, you will also need to refrain from introducing entirely different topics. If it's a different topic, it deserves its own email or conversation.

Make sure that your communication is complete and coherent. If you don't include complete information in the beginning, it slows down the communication process. Likewise, if your communication isn't coherent you are likely to lose your audience's attention. A coherent message is logical, all of the points you are trying to make are connected and relevant to the main topic of conversation while the tone and flow of the content is consistent. While being coherent, a complete message must contain all of the relevant information; think who, what, when, where, why and how as necessary depending on the type of message being conveyed. The most needful point of your message should be the call to action. Tell your reader or listener exactly what you want them to do and why it's important for them to do it.

Finally, make sure that you are being courteous to the recipient. Not being courteous is a great way to ensure that you are treated rudely. This is often the biggest mistake that people make, and can quickly shut down communication on a negative note.

Great communication should answer the five W's used by journalists when they write a story. It should tell who, what, when, where and why. While communicating, ensure that you are clear, concise, complete, coherent and courteous.

Depending upon with whom you are communicating, it will be important to carefully choose how you communicate your message. If there is any chance that you need to discuss any information that is confidential, then you need to control who can hear that information. Remember that people love to spread information that they have no need to know in the first place, so you need to take steps to control who knows the information in the first place. Remember that many companies have their own privacy policies but that there are also laws in place, such as HIPAA, that can and often do take precedence over individual companies. These policies and laws are in place to protect not only the one sending the messages but also the ones about whom those messages are sent. Even in your personal communications, you will want to expose potentially sensitive information to public scrutiny. It can embarrass not only the subject of your discussion but yourself as well if the wrong people find out about it.

Develop Self-Confidence to Communicate Effectively

Dale Carnegie in his best-selling book How to Win Friends and Influence People says that a person's success in life is determined 85 percent by their ability to lead others, and only 15 percent by what people know. There is absolutely no place where this statement is more evident than when it comes to communication.

In order to lead people, you must have enough self-confidence to put yourself last as you serve other people. Therefore, it is essential to understand the process of developing self-confidence if you want to be an effective communicator.

If you need to communicate with someone and you are feeling hesitant, there are some tricks that you can use to appear more confident when communicating. The first of these tricks is to dress sharper. You do not have to have the newest clothes, but pay special attention that they are well cared for as it is a great way to show others how much you care about your appearance.

Another trick is to change your stride. How you walk can influence how you are seen. Whether you walk slightly faster than you do already or in a more upright fashion, people will notice. Numerous studies show that people who walk faster are perceived as more important than those who walk at a slower pace. It is also known that people who walk with shoulders back and a longer stride are less likely to be accosted on the street. Therefore, you can influence how your message is perceived simply by putting some pep in your step. Of course, because you are anxious to complete your life goals, you are anxious to complete your goals.

In order to appear to have more self-confidence, practice good posture. Keep your shoulders back and your head held high. Make sure to look the person that you are communicating with in the eyes. This tends to make the other person more confident in your abilities which will give your own self-confidence a boost.

If you need to build your self-confidence, listen to a motivational podcast or find an inspirational message online. Everyone is motivated by different messages, but a few people that you may want to consider listening to include Eric Thomas, Les Brown, Tony Robbins, Nick Vujicic, Zig Ziglar and Dr. Wayne Dyer.

When you are feeling particularly timid, then try creating a gratitude list. Simply grab a piece of paper and make a list of all the things that you are most grateful for in the world. In fact, researchers know that setting aside a portion of each week to write in a gratitude journal has amazing results.

Guard yourself from speaking negatively about yourself as well as other people. Your mother really was right, if you do not have something positive to say about someone, then say nothing at all. The effect of saying negative things about others is not only that you tear down their self-worth, but you destroy your own as well. The Chinese general and strategist said, "Know yourself and you will win all battles." This includes the battles you will fight with yourself when you feel those negative thoughts cropping up. Imagine each negative thought as a bug and then stomp on it, mentally of course. Once you've squashed that negative though out of existence, replace it with something positive. Be vigilant about watching for these negative bugs, they will creep out when you least expect it.

If you are delaying communicating a message, then it really is time that you speak up. Ninety percent of the time, you will discover that people respect you more when you take a stand even if they do not agree with your point of view. Realizing this greatly enhances your self-worth.

People who work out on a regular basis are much more likely to feel better about themselves. When a person works out, the body produces happy hormones that naturally makes a person feel better. Therefore, make sure that you are planning a time to work out on a regular basis regardless of how busy your schedule.

Finally, you must realize that each person makes an important contribution to the overall success of a project. That includes you. Therefore, make sure to feel pride in your contribution to any project.

Now that you are feeling confident about yourself, you are in a much better position to communicate with others. Start each communication with praise and honest appreciation. Everyone that you communicate with does something very well. Identify what you like about that person first and last. If you must deliver a negative message, then put it in the middle. Soften the blow by giving them a compliment before suggesting that there is something they've done that isn't exactly what you were asking for.

Never tell someone directly that they are making a mistake. Instead, tell the person that their work might be better for another purpose. The Dallas Cowboys, one of the best football teams in America, practices this effectively when they must get rid of a player. They call the player into the office without any other people around and tell the player that they are not right for their organization. They then tell the player that they really hope that they find a team where their skills will be useful. Since they have not told the player that they do not have any skills, many players have gone home, worked on their skills, and come back to successfully play for another team.

If you bark orders, then people get their feelings hurt. Instead, of barking orders, use questions to encourage others to do what you need them to do. Do not allow yourself to become a drill sergeant in an army. Instead, figure out how to ask questions that will get people to do what you want them to do.

Let's assume that you are leading a team project and one of your employees is not doing what he needs to do on time. Yet, the employee comes to you wanting to take a long weekend off. Instead of telling him no, see if you can come up with a solution that will make you both happy. Start by asking if the employee's work has been completed. Even though you know the answer, this gives the employee the chance to tell you the truth. Then, ask what it would take to get the work complete. In many situations, it does not matter when the work is done, but that it is done. This also allows you to be certain that the employee has the resources needed to complete the job. Using questions to allow people to come up with their own solutions ensures that you are creating a win-win situation.

Good communication allows the other person to save face. Everyone has areas of weakness. Sometimes these areas must be addressed. Therefore, think about how you can do it so that the other person can save face. Many conversations become argumentative, because of one person's desire to put another person down. Do not fall into this trap. Think of a way that allows the other person to save face in every conversation even if they are wrong.

In order to do this, time your conversation very carefully. A conversation that happens in haste often leaves the other person angry. Be very clear about your intentions by showing the other person that you really do have their best interest at heart. While you may have very strong opinions on a subject, make sure to stick to the facts. Make sure that you do not consider your opinions fact. Leave yourself open to the possibility that other things may be occurring that you do not see.

Make sure that you are being an active listener. Pay attention to what the other person has to say. Use good eye contact, and smile as often as possible. Watch to see if the person you are addressing starts to mirror your body language. If they are messing with their phones or are otherwise occupying themselves, then assume that they are not actively listening.

There are also important clues that you can watch for to make sure that your messages are being received in a positive way. Often times, these clues are much more subtle than the eye roll that a teenager gives his parents. Start by watching to make sure that the arms stay close to the body and that the listener's hands stay in a natural position. Most times that the person who crosses their arms in front of them are not hearing your message or accepting it. Angry people often have very minimal facial expressions, and the listener will not be looking at you. If the person even subtly turns away from you, then you can assume the person is not listening.

It may seem like a person that you are trying to help may make two steps forward and six steps back. Therefore, it is important to praise even the slightest improvement and every improvement that you see after that. Find ways to praise the person that they will appreciate and you will soon find the other person is working even harder to make you happy.

If you must deliver a tough message, then make sure to give the other person time to digest the information. Check back with them after a day or so to see if they have any additional information or questions that they want to discuss. While staying true to your own message, find a place in your heart to truly care about the other individual.

The old adage is really true, when you are pointing your finger at someone else, realize that you have three fingers pointing back at yourself. Therefore, before you communicate, make sure that you are attending to your own business. Everyone has weaknesses, so take steps to identify your weaknesses and let those around you see that you are working on them.

The Art of Small Talk

Before you communicate with another individual, it is important to know who is listening. A great way to do that is to use small talk. These conversations happen all the time and are crucial to networking with others. It is important to be good at small talk because it allows you to foster relationships and build communities.

The first key to having a great time at a networking event is to set your expectations very low. If you come to an event expecting nothing more than a recommendation on where to go on vacation or what restaurant to eat in next, then you can relax. When you are relaxed, you are usually at your best.

Woody Morcott, owner of the Dana Corporation which does business in 29 different countries, stresses that it is important to dress so that you are approachable at networking events. Since he feels that many of his employees may be unwilling to approach him because of his position, he always wears a humorous tie to these events. The tie automatically gives people something to talk to him about. Once the conversation is started, then he is able to capitalize on the time spent with his employees and colleagues to hear what he has to tell him.

Sam Walton used a slightly different approach when he was starting Walmart and for many years later. When visiting his stores he always drove an old red pickup and usually wore an old baseball cap. He almost always wore a white short sleeve shirt. He did all this to make himself more approachable.

If you know the names of some of the people that will be at the networking event, then spend a little time ahead of the event finding out something about some of the people that will be there. There are many different places that you can find this information. One way is to just search their name and see what pops up about them. In this time, most people have a Linked-In account and that can be a great place to find out information. For example, you can see if you and the person have any friends in common or have attended any of the same universities. Likewise, you can mine their Facebook account for information. Doing all this helps you find things to talk about when you meet them.

Go into a networking event armed with information that you can talk about during the event. In particular, think about answers to common questions that you are likely to encounter such as how are you and how things are going. Preparing more than one word answers to these common questions ahead of time further allows you to relax. It also allows you to be more interesting and gives the person asking the question several choices on how they can follow up on your comments.

Come prepared to start a conversation with a declarative statement. When you open with a question, you may accidentally ask about the one topic that a person does not want to talk about. Instead, lead with a declarative statement such as "I watched a great movie the other night called The Ballad of Narayama that told about a girl in Japan." This gives the other person the opportunity to share their opinion of the film with you if they have seen it. Alternatively, they can choose to tell you about a great movie that they have watched. They can also choose to tell you about their trip to Japan.

Once you have started talking with an individual, then follow up with questions about themselves. People generally love to talk about themselves, so this is an easy way to move the conversation forward. As you find common ground, then expand on those topics. This allows you to talk about a subject that you enjoy and are knowledgeable about and a topic that others are interested in as well.

Your body language says a lot about how approachable you are during a networking event. Make sure that you keep your arms and hands hanging loosely by your body.

Do not cross them in front of you as this gives the appearance that you are not open to what the other person is saying. Additionally, make sure that you keep your legs in a natural position. If you are standing, do not lock your knees, as it gives you an awkward appearance that makes you seem unapproachable. If seated, then either keep both feet flat on the floor or fold one leg over the other. The foot should dangle toward the person who is leading the conversation in most cases.

Follow up with 'I' statements as often as possible. These statements allow the other individual to know that you are listening. As much as possible, interject humor into the situation to show that you have a great sense of humor.

When attending a networking event, make sure to talk to many different people. This allows you to meet even more people. Realize that the goal of a networking event is to develop contacts. If someone really seems to interest you, then see if you can set up a meeting with them later. In no case, however, should you become a wall flower during these events. Staying in the corner and not visiting with anyone or just a couple of friends that came with you should not be an option at a networking event.

When meeting new people make sure to repeat the person's name and then use it early in the conversation.

Not only do people love to hear their names, but it also reinforces the name in your mind. Most importantly, however, it helps you know that you heard the name correctly in the first place.

It is helpful when attending networking events to be well read in current events. People often have strong opinions on these events. Having a strong opinion, however, does not mean that you have to voice it loudly. Be open to listening to other people's ideas, and see where there is common ground between your ideas and their ideas.

Networking events are scary to many people, but they need not be that way. Prepare ahead of time with topics that you think other people would be interested in learning about. Stay open to mingling with many people at these events. Enjoy them by setting very low expectations and then anything that you take away from the event will be an added bonus.

Gulp! I have to Give a Presentation

At some point in time almost everyone has to give a presentation. Many people freeze up during these times and cannot think what to say or do. Yet, making a great presentation can be very important to succeeding in the workplace. Just like being an effective speaker, creating an effective presentation will make the best use of the relationship between you and your audience.

It is important to plan any presentation before you give it. If it is a more informal presentation, then you may be able to just create a list of ideas. If it is a more formal presentation, then it is best to write out the presentation. Depending on the situation, you may even want to memorize it or create a power point for your audience to follow along. Take the time to put your presentation in a logical order that is easy for the audience to follow. If you are using technology, such as a Power Point, make sure that it is working properly before starting your speech.

Your presentation should take into consideration your audience's needs in order to capture their interest, inspire their confidence, and help to develop their understanding as well as achieve your particular objectives. Therefore, if you find it necessary to give a presentation, then follow these simple tips to create a successful presentation.

First you need to prepare yourself for giving that presentation. As you begin making notes on what you want your final preparation to look like, you will want to bear in mind exactly what you want to achieve and what you want your audience to take away with them. Making definitive decisions on what your objectives are, you will be in a much better position to make decisions about the design and tone of your presentation. Questions to ask at this stage are; 'What do you want your audience to understand?' 'Do you want your audience to take action after your presentation? If so, what is it?' and 'How can you design your presentation so that you can meet your objectives?'

You will want to think about the best format for your speech. A popular technique that works for many people is start by telling the audience where you were when you started on the journey that you are going to talk about. Then, move on to talking about the steps that you took on the journey. Finally, tell the audience where you are today.

For example, let's pretend that you are Bill Gates in about 2000. He might begin his presentation with how he started out making $20,000 from Traf-o-Data. Then, he could move on to where he is today. The final part of the presentation would be the details about how he got to be one of the wealthiest businessmen in the world.

When you have determined your objectives, now you are ready to think more in-depth about your audience. They will have a variety of different interests, experiences and levels of knowledge. You will need to acknowledge these and be ready to respond to them accordingly. Questions to ask yourself about your audience are; 'How much do they already know about the topic?' 'Can you link new material to things they already understand?' and 'Do you need to win them over to a particular point of view?"

While you might not be able to answer all of these questions for each member of your audience, you should still have enough information to allow you to present your material at a level where the entire audience will be able to understand it. For example, if you are a teacher talking to a group of teachers, then you can use words like IEP, learning objective, deductive thinking, and inductive thinking. Alternatively, if you are talking to a group of parents, then you may have to explain what each of these terms mean or avoid them altogether. If you don't consider your audience's needs then you will fail to appeal to their interests and spark their imaginations.

Once you know your objectives and who your audience is, you need to address your venue. Where you are making your presentation and what the room is like will help you to create the kind of atmosphere you want for your information. Whether you are asked to make a presentation or you are giving one for work or church, there are some questions that you can ask when arranging a venue. 'What kind of atmosphere do you want to create?' 'Can the room be arranged to positively effect your relationship with your audience and suit your objectives?' and 'Are audio-visual aids available and will they make a difference to the material you are presenting?'

While you are considering your venue, you will want to determine if the people you are making this presentation to or the location you are using have any time constraints. Certain places may have rented out the room that you are making your presentation in after yours is concluded. Perhaps the people who are your audience are only available for a short period of time. Both of these will effect how you plan your presentation. Be certain that you know how much time you have been allowed for your presentation.

When the preparation for your presentation has been made, you begin the real work of planning. Your second task is to define your main points. You should try not to present more than three main points if you are limited to a ten minute presentation. However, remember that you must allow an adequate amount of time for both an introduction and conclusion to your presentation. Unless you provide a significant amount of assistance, your audience will find it very difficult to follow a more complex presentation. Ask these questions when writing out your main points; 'What are your main points?' 'Are your main points structured logically and coherently?' 'Do your main points reflect the objectives you want to achieve?' and 'Are you taking the needs of your audience into account?'

Your third task is when you develop your supporting information that will help your audience to understand and agree with the points being made in your presentation. Your evidence may take the form of factual data or a more complex explanation of processes. You can offer this information in a variety of imaginative ways by using diagrams, graphs, pictures, anecdotes or video segments. When you are dealing with supporting information, you want to use only what will add clarity and authority to your arguments.

The next stage in planning your presentation is to be certain that there is a linear flow to your points. You can achieve this by using linking statements to clearly show how your main points fit together. These linking statements help your audience follow each main objective since they highlight the next point in your argument while linking to earlier ideas and clarifying the final point of your presentation. This is particularly important if your presentation is long and more complex because it will help to keep your audience involved and attentive.

Finally, you are finished making notes and are finally ready to actually write your presentation down as if you were writing an essay or a letter. As with an essay or letter, both the introduction and conclusion are crucial for a successful presentation. The introduction is your first point of contact with your audience and it is where you will either capture or lose their interest. You must start your presentation with a bang. If you do not hook your audience in the first 30 seconds, then you have probably lost them forever.

You want to use your introduction to lay a clear path for your presentation to follow. An introduction to a presentation is similar to a thesis statement but it is expanded somewhat to introduce yourself as well as your topic. Unlike a thesis statement, an introduction will use future tense verbiage rather than past or present tense. You can use the following as a standard structure for developing your introduction; introduce yourself and your topic, tell your audience how you will be presenting your information, what you intend the outcome to be and what you expect your audience to do. Before launching into your first main point you will want to give your listeners a moment to absorb the information you have given them.

Many people believe that a conclusion is just the opposite of an introduction but it isn't when either writing or speaking. When giving a presentation, your conclusion is just as critical as your introduction because you are summarizing your entire presentation into simplified words to allow your audience to remember what they have already heard during your more complex presentation. While the introduction used future tense words, the conclusion will use past tense words since you are reminding your audience of what has just occurred during your presentation.

The conclusion should be short and powerful. It should be something that the audience will remember if they remember nothing else from your speech. A powerful conclusion follows a general structure of review, summary, concluding statement and a parting statement. The review section reminds your listeners about the title or subject matter that has been discussed. The summary is basically a listing of the main points as well as the process you took them through. The concluding statement is clearly drawn from your main points and usually only includes the first and last points and the relationship, or lack thereof, between those points. Your parting statement should stimulate your audience's thoughts or imagination and is often referred to as the 'call to action' though it can be formed as a question or a bold comment. If you want the audience to take specific actions after the presentation, then make sure to tell them exactly what you want them to do, as more people will follow through if they think there is something in it for them.

If you are including a question and answer period at the end of your presentation, then think about any questions that might get asked that you are not prepared to answer at this time. No one can think of every question that might be asked during a question and answer period so you may find yourself needing to 'think on your feet' to come up with a professional and courteous way to tell them you will have to get back to them with the answer. Have a pen and paper available so that you can get their contact information and let them know exactly when you will follow up. Be sure to follow up when you say you will!

Even if you use a question and answer period to end your presentation, it is still important to make a closing statement. Something as simple as, 'That is all I have for today.' works if you have done a conclusion before the question and answer.

It cannot be stressed enough that the last 30 seconds of your speech is nearly as important as the first. Therefore, make sure to close on a high note. Make sure to leave your audience feeling full of energy and excited about your presentation.

And now, once you have written your presentation you are ready to review its content. A few more questions and you are ready to practice your presentation to find exactly the right tone of voice and body language to use during the presentation. While reviewing your written presentation, ask yourself the following; 'Does it meet your objectives?' 'Has it been structured logically and coherently?' 'Is the material targeted at the right level for the audience?' and 'Does it meet the time allotment?' As with any communication, if you answer 'no' to any of these questions during the review period then you must go back and change anything that needs to be changed so that you can answer 'yes' to all questions.

After you have planned your presentation, especially a formal one, make sure to practice giving it. Make sure that if you need to fill a particular time slot that your speech achieves that goal. It is usually best to give the speech in front of one or two of your friends first, but if that is not possible, then give the speech in front of a mirror or videotape your speech. Giving your presentation to friends or so that you can see yourself will allow you to adjust your nonverbal communication just as the review period of your written presentation allows you to adjust and refine the information you are presenting.

Regardless of whether you are giving a formal or informal presentation, you need to create rapport with your audience. The most important piece of advice that you can ever receive in building a rapport with your audience comes from Oscar Wilde who said, "Be yourself. Everyone else is taken."

Even if you take Oscar Wilde's advice and are being yourself, you may feel yourself experiencing pre-presentation jitters. This is perfectly fine since many people experience stage fright even when they have given presentations before. In fact, some people become worried that they have not put enough emphasis on the speech if they are not nervous right before it begins. There are many ways that you can handle these pre-speech jitters. Some of the most popular include visualizing yourself at your best, repeating positive affirmations about yourself, deep breathing, and virtual reality therapy.

If you are giving a presentation for the first time, the following tips will help you to seem more confident. They will also help you during your practice so that you get used to using these techniques with your audience.

Your introduction is where you will build rapport with your listeners. There are numerous ways that you can build rapport with your audience. One way that is often used is to start your presentation with a humorous joke or story. This helps the audience relax and prepare themselves to hear what else you have to say. It is important that you use humor appropriately. Make sure that it relates to the rest of your presentation and is appropriate to your audience.

Asking a question is also a good way to build rapport with an audience. It can be a real question that the audience probably already knows the answer to or it can be a rhetorical question. After asking the question, then be sure to pause and give the audience time to answer.

You want to be sure to seem to be looking your audience directly in the eyes. If you are nervous and find this difficult to do, then pick a point right above their heads and look at that spot. The audience usually never suspects that you are not looking them square in the eyes, and it often helps you to relax.

Giving a public presentation can be scary for everyone. In fact, many professional speakers and actors report that they are still a little nervous before each speech. It is best that you make sure to plan your speech well ahead of time so that it communicates effectively with your audience. When planning your speech consider telling your audience where you started, where you are now, and how you got to your present place. Use language throughout the speech that connects with your audience. Practice your speech, and if you are using technology make sure that it works properly. In particular, make sure you capture the audience's attention in the first 30 seconds and leave them feeling energized.

Communicating Through Letter Writing

If you are writing a letter, the process should basically be the same. Being able to write a coherent letter is an essential skill even in today's world where emails and text messages are prevalent. You never know when you will need to write a letter of complaint or a cover letter for your resume to an employer. Writing letters can help to improve your communication as well as social skills.

As mentioned before, you cannot really understand someone's meaning if you can't take in both the verbal and nonverbal communication of a speaker. Conversely, your listener has the same difficulty. This is why tone of voice is so important when speaking on the telephone. However, letter writing as well as the more common text and email messages require you to express those nonverbal cues in a purely verbal manner. Don't be mistaken, the written word is still considered verbal communication despite it not being spoken. Understanding your purpose behind writing your letter will help you to determine the goal you want to achieve through that letter. Knowing how to write in a logical and coherent fashion is essential for your success when communicating through the written word.

The first step in writing a good letter or email is to identify why you are writing it in the first place. Write that purpose out on a piece of scratch paper because you will need to refer to it often as you are completing your work. Make it as concise as possible.

Now that you have identified the reason that you are writing, then think about your target audience. In most cases, that will be the group or individual that you are addressing in your letter. Knowing who you are writing to will allow you to identify the language your target audience will identify with more easily.

There are two different letter formats; business and personal. Make sure to choose the format that is right for your situation. A personal letter will be written to friends, family members and other people that you know well enough to be on a first name basis with. Business letters are much more formal and use more formal language. Below is a brief overview of who you would outline both personal and business letters.

Structure of a Personal Letter

- Your address as the sender should always appear in the top right hand corner of the page. Many people will also include the date the letter is written before including their return address.

- Though it is not often the case, sometimes you may want to include your email and telephone numbers beneath the return address on the right hand side of the page beneath your address.

- The greeting will vary depending upon who you are writing to and how well you know the person. Examples are; Dear Mary, Hello, or Greetings.

- The body will contain all of the information you are wanting to convey. Remember to give each topic within the letter its own paragraph so that it is easier for the other person to read rather than giving them a wall of text.

- While all letters end with a complimentary close or valediction, personal letters tend to be more affectionate in nature. For example; Love, Lots of love, With thanks, or See you soon.

Structure of Business Letters

- These letters are always written on an 8"x11" sheet of paper which is also called an A4. This is so that they can be folded three times so that the recipients address can appear in the window of a business envelope.

- Unlike a personal letter, in a business letter the senders address including telephone number and email address as necessary appears in the top left hand corner above the recipient's address.

- The date is always included in a business letter. It should be situated between the sender's and recipient's addresses with a line skipped if the letter is being typed with single spacing.

- The address of the recipient appears below the date.

- The greeting will usually be Dear Sir or Dear Madam. If you know the name of the person to whom you are writing, you can use Miss, Mrs. or Mr. followed by their last name. Sometimes you won't know exactly who will be reading your letter. In this case, you can open your letter with To Whom It May Concern to avoid offending anyone.

- The body of your letter is the same as for the personal letter though with more formal language and style. Your introductory paragraph tells your reader why you are writing to them. The following paragraphs will highlight your objectives just as if you were giving a presentation though more succinctly. The last paragraph is your conclusion;

this is where you summarize what you wrote about and thank the reader for their time and attention.

- Again, you will have a complimentary close, or valediction, of a more formal nature such as; Yours faithfully, Cordially or Sincerely.

- The business letter has two 'sign-offs'. The first is your written signature that is unique to you and is usually written in cursive with whatever flourish is your individual trademark. Below that you will need to write in block letters your full name so that if your signature is not fully legible they will know who is signing the letter.

Once you know how you should lay out your letter and the purpose behind writing it, you are ready to sit down and actually write.

If you are writing a personal letter to a family member or close friend, you may want to ask them how they are initially and assure them that you are doing well too. This is perfectly fine, but you should state the purpose for your letter directly after that so they aren't wondering why you are writing to them. This statement is like writing a thesis statement of an essay. It gives a specific explanation and tells the reader what the rest of the letter will be about. The remainder of your letter should support this statement. It often helps to think of it as a road map that shows you where you want to go.

Each paragraph should engage the audience and further support your thesis statement. In most cases, do not write more than two pages. Make sure to adjust the tone to address the exact group of people or person that you are addressing in the letter. The language that you use will help you to set the tone of your message in a business letter. This is where the skills you read about earlier in this book come back into play. You need to consider the age, gender and culture your reader will identify with so that you do not accidentally offend or confuse them with the words you choose to use.

When writing, try to put yourself in the reader's position. You want to make your point so that they understand exactly what you are trying to accomplish. This helps to ensure that they see things from your viewpoint as much as possible.

The closing paragraph of your letter should both summarize your letter's intent, state exactly what you hope that the reader will do and to thank them for their time and attention. You want to tell them specifically how you hope that they will respond. Keep your closing paragraph short, no longer than three or four sentences.

When you have concluded your letter, you can close with the proper valediction and sign your name.

There are at least three types of letters that require special attention. The first of these is the cover letter that you should write to accompany every resume. Cover letters fall into three different types. They can be sent when you are applying to a specific job that the company has open. They can also be sent when you are asking if there are any openings at the company that might meet your qualifications. Finally, they can be sent when you are asking someone to help you find a job by recommending you. You will need to make sure that your cover letter is personalized for each purpose and for each company.

The best way to determine how to write a cover letter for a specific company is to find out as much as you can about the company where you are applying or looking for openings. With today's technology, it is easy to search for and find information on specific companies whether it is through Linked-In or on a company website. The level of formality on these sites will give you a guide as to how formal your tone should be when writing a letter to a specific company. However, at the same time, it is vitally important that you be yourself in the letter as well.

You will want to use the body of the letter to show the employer what you can do for them. The cover letter should be kept extremely short. In total, you should try to use less than 200 words. The employer can potentially receive hundreds of cover letters in a day, so it is important to write a letter that they can read in under 30 seconds. Because of this necessity you must be able to write an extremely powerful letter that is to the point to capture your reader's attention and hopefully capitalize on that interest.

You must believe that you are the best applicant for the position. Then, you must show the person reading the letter that this statement is true. You should never cover all of the information appearing on your resume in your cover letter; however, you should highlight the most important facts. Put yourself in the potential employer's place and choose details that you think will impress him or her.

When opening your cover letter, don't waste time on useless pleasantries. You want to use the very first sentence of your letter to state why they are reading the letter. If you are writing for a particular position you will want to state that very specifically. If you are writing to ask about potential job openings, then you want to state that as well. It is important to remember that if you are requesting return information that you make the reply the potential employer will be making as simple as possible. If you make it too difficult they are more likely to ignore your request. This may necessitate including a self-addressed stamped envelope for them to use.

You will want to use the second paragraph of your letter to briefly summarize the highlights of your career that qualifies you for the position. This should be highly relevant and not tell your life's journey. Remember not to ramble, get straight to the point and then move on.

Use the third paragraph to state exactly why you feel that you are the best qualified candidate. This is where you would include information on how you can provide value to your reader's company if you were to be hired. Again, you must be very specific, keep it brief and, above all, make it powerful.

The last paragraph of your letter should tell the person reading the letter exactly how you would like them to follow up. Despite being on your resume, use this paragraph to state your phone number and your email address. If you would like something in writing, then this is where you would request that courtesy and point out the inclusion of the self-addressed stamped envelope for their use. Then, close the letter with the proper valediction.

The second type of letter that you may need to write is a letter of resignation. Despite how you may be feeling about the position, this letter is not the place to state those feelings or air grievances. In most cases, these letters should only be two paragraphs long. In some cases, they can be two sentences long.

The first paragraph should clearly state what position you are resigning from and give your last work date. If you plan to take any accrued vacation or other personal time during what can be considered 'two-week notice', then make sure to state that fact too.

The second paragraph of the letter should thank the company for letting you work there. Even if you do not feel thankful, you still need to write a sentence or two that shows why you are thankful for the opportunity and perhaps what you have learned during your tenure in your position. Then, sign your name. There really is no need to air any complaints that you have about the company or personnel.

The third type of letter that you may need to write at some point is a letter of recommendation. If you cannot recommend someone, then it is important to tell them instead of trying to lie in your letter. Before attempting to write the letter, you should arm yourself with as much information about the position and the person you are being asked to recommend as you possibly can.

Letters of recommendation should be written using the business format. The first two or three lines are used to introduce yourself, to state why you are qualified to write the letter and inform the reader exactly who you are recommending to them and their company.

If you are a former employer, the second paragraph will state what the person's position in your company was, whether or not you supervised them and the person's leaving salary. You will want to include how long the person was employed by your company. This is where you will reference the skills, qualities, areas of knowledge and other assets of the person you are recommending. You will want to convey the strengths the applicant possesses by citing examples of tasks and accomplishments they performed while at your company.

If you are a professor writing this letter, in the second paragraph you would state the course the person took and what grade they received. You would want to convey your thoughts on the student's scholarly capabilities as well as their personal character as well. If you are writing a letter of recommendation for a student to apply for a job in the field you teach in, then you will also want to include information on pertinent extra-curricular activities the student took part in that would enhance their skills and experience.

If you are writing a personal recommendation, then state how you know the individual, the length of time you have known the person you are recommending and what you perceive to be their personal character. This is often the most difficult type of recommendation letter to write since you may not be aware of their strengths within a particular industry.

No matter the type of recommendation letter you are writing, your closing paragraph would include your desire to hire the person again along with a positive statement about your belief that the person being recommended would be an outstanding addition to the reader's staff.

Many people feel that letter writing is a lost art. It need not be that way. Learning to write a powerful, coherent letter shows that you know the value or your words.

Hostile Communication

So far in this guide, we have focused mainly on communicating in the business environment. There will be times in your life that you may want to communicate socially with the opposite sex. Men really are wired differently than women, so there are several facts that you will want to keep in mind.

One person is often more able to share their feelings verbally than another person. Usually, but not always, it is the woman. It is very important that if you are the verbal one that you slow down and let the other person be able to process what information you are providing. A great way to do this is to ask statements encouraging the other person to repeat back to you what they think that you said. This not only gives them time to process the information, but ensures that you are delivering the message that you think you are delivering.

When you are angry, it can be very difficult to not have an angry face. Yet, a research study conducted by the University of South Carolina found that when a person sees an angry face, they are less able to process information. This same study found that men are much less likely to be able to read facial expressions, and feel empathy toward them.

While everyone has heard that it is important to walk away from a hostile situation, the opposite may be true, according to researchers. In fact, continually being angry, and not expressing those feelings, can be as detrimental to one's heart as smoking.

It is vital to remember the five Cs when you are angry. Keeping these Cs in mind helps ensure that when you are done, the two of you can still be friends.

The first C is to be courteous. While you may want to say many things that are not positive, chances are that you will regret it later. Therefore, make sure to say what is on your mind using a method that allows the other person to leave the conversation with their self-worth still intact.

The second C is to be concise. While it may be very tempting to dredge up something that the other person did last week or last year that made you angry, you need to stick to the point of the current disagreement. Take a few moments to understand exactly why you are angry before you start the conversation.

The third C is to be clear about your message. Unfortunately, this is the most difficult C to achieve in the heat of the moment. Especially if your brain is sizzling and flitting from one slight to the next like a hyperactive bumble bee gathering pollen. When you are angry, there is no need to drop subtle clues. Instead, you should be very explicit about why you are angry. The best way to do this is to use 'I' statements that tells the other person how you are feeling.

Before you begin take a moment to think about what you what you want the other person to do, and then deliver that message. This allows the other person to respond to exactly what you want them to do. If this step is not completed, then the other person may totally miss the message. This is why arguments continue past the initial disagreements, it's just not easy to think coherently much less speak coherently when emotions are running high.

The fourth C is to be cognizance. You need to be aware of how the other person is receiving your message. Experts recommend that you listen at least 75 percent as much as you talk. In fact, many decades ago, the Jews had a proverb that said that there was a reason that the tongue, representing words, was hidden behind a row of teeth, because the teeth provided a defensive wall to stop the words that should not be said. Again, along with being clear, this is very difficult to accomplish when you are angry. Depending upon the culture you are from, you may spend 80 to 90 percent of the time talking and yelling over the person with whom you are arguing. This lack of listening often leads to lingering disagreements and misunderstandings.

The final C is to claim yourself. You need to understand who you are and how what happened affects how you are feeling. Instead of placing blame on another individual, you should tell the other person how you are feeling and thinking. This is often accompanied by tears rather than anger so it is a little easier to be clear in your communication though coherency can still suffer.

It is very important to remember that you communicate in many different ways. This is especially true when you are having a hostile conversation. Therefore, make sure to think about the volume of your voice. Decide to make a conscious effort to keep it lower than normal. This helps the other person concentrate on what you are saying as well as helping to diffuse a tense situation.

It is also important to control the pitch of your voice. Many people, especially women, talk much higher in pitch when they are angry. The higher pitched tones of voice can cause physical pain especially during an emotionally tense situation since anger causes blood pressure to rise. This phenomena causes the nerves of the inner ear vibrate due to the close proximity of pulsing blood vessels. You should try to make a conscious effort to control the pitch of your voice to ensure that the other person does not cringe just from hearing your voice and is able to hear your message.

Additionally, many people talk much faster when they are angry. Therefore, you need to develop techniques that allow you to control the cadence of your voice. Practice speaking slowly. Try to keep your body language open. If you find yourself clenching your teeth or your fist, then take a moment to breathe deeply and relax.

It is equally important to make sure that you are controlling your tone. There are several concrete things that you can do to make sure that your tone does not become too harsh. Start by making sure that you are breathing from the diaphragm. Make sure that you are sitting or standing up straight, because it makes it easier to breathe correctly.

A great way to make sure that you are controlling your voice correctly is to enunciate your words carefully. Slurring your words only makes it more difficult for other people to understand exactly what you are trying to say. You want to make sure that you are putting the endings on all of your words. Additionally, be certain that your words contain all of their syllables.

There are times in everyone's life when they must deliver a hostile message. Before you start your message, make sure that you are being courteous to the other individual. Be concise about your message, and focus it clearly on what is making your angry at the moment. Remember that the other person has feelings, so make sure that you are cognizant about how you are making them feel. Finally, make sure to claim yourself. A great way to do all of this is to control your volume, pitch, fluency, tone and enunciation.

Fitting All the Pieces Together

It is essential to remember that your communication has many different pieces. In this book, we have dealt with the way that you deliver your message and what message that you need to be delivering. Before we close, however, it is essential to touch on the other elements of communication.

The first of these is gestures. A mother and a daughter often can carry on a whole conversation across a crowded room using only gestures. Gestures are unique to the individual. Most gestures should be kept small unless you are on a stage making a point. Concentrating on your message should allow your gestures to come naturally. If you are having trouble communicating your message, then make sure that your message and your gestures are matching.

Eye contact is another important element of communication. According to Michigan State University, the more that you look a person in the eye, the more dominant you will appear. You will also appear more credible. Alternatively, looking away, especially down, is a sign of being submissive. If you are angry, then try not to stare at the other individual.

It is also important to control your posture to communicate effectively. Folded arms or crossed legs makes you appear very aggressive and defensive. Therefore, it is essential to avoid this position to ensure that your message is effectively received. Instead, make sure that you keep your elbows slightly away from your body and arms in a natural position with your fingers spread slightly apart. In order to be taken seriously, make sure that your shoulders are kept slightly back and your head held in an upright position. If you want the other person to know that you are very interested in what they have to say, then lean slightly towards that individual. Alternatively, if you want to reduce the tensions while communicating try leaning slightly backwards.

If you want to lift up a mood at a meeting, then dress sharply. Research shows that wearing blue jeans or baggy clothes is perceived as being depressed. Wear shoes that you can walk comfortably in as they give the listener the perception that you have a lot of energy. Believe it or not, women wearing bright red lipstick made more money than those who wore a more subtle tone. Aim to present yourself in your best possible light.

When your message seems to be falling on deaf ears, then make sure to check your facial expressions. While it may be very difficult to deliver some messages without crying, research shows that it actually makes your message harder to hear. Researchers are not sure why, but the left side of the face shows more emotion than the right side. In short, make sure that your facial expressions line up with your message.

There are many ways that your body needs to align with your spoken words. Make sure to use small gestures that are not perceived as hostile in any way. Look your intended audience in the eyes to make sure that your message is getting through, unless you want to appear submissive, then look slightly down. Keep your body language open and you will have a better chance of your message being heard. Dress sharply to make sure that your message to present an uplifting mood in any meeting. Finally, make sure that your facial expressions are matching your message.

Conclusion

You have reached the end of this book. I want to thank you for reading it. Hopefully, you have learned a lot about communication in its many different forms including asking appropriate questions and developing the self-confidence needed to speak in any situation.

You also learned how to communicate in many different situations. You have learned how to communicate at networking events, how to give a presentation, and how to communicate when writing a letter.

Finally, you have learned how to communicate when you must deliver a hostile message and how your non-verbal communication needs to match your message.

If you have enjoyed this message, then we only ask two favors of you. First, make sure to tell a friend how much you enjoyed reading this book and recommend that they read it too. Secondly, we ask that you leave a review so that others will know how much you enjoyed reading this book. It is often through your feedback that people decide what they want to read.

Remember that communication takes more than one person. When you do your part, however, you are better able to deliver your message. The rest is up to the other people. As you practice the skills in this book, and improve your skills, you are doing your part.

Made in the USA
San Bernardino, CA
13 May 2016